Egyptian Mythology

A Guide to Egyptian History, Gods,

and Mythology

Peter Collins

Table of Contents

Introduction 1

Chapter 1: The Might of Egypt 4

Chapter 2: Life in Ancient Egypt... 12

Chapter 3: The Egyptian Creation Myth.................................... 16

Chapter 4: Egyptian Gods and Goddesses 24

Chapter 5: Egyptian Monsters and Other Stories 42

Chapter 6: Temples of the Gods... 51

Conclusion 65

Introduction

Before there was Christianity, Judaism, or Islam, there was polytheistic religion, which we now refer to as mythology. Functionally though, mythology is just a religion that has gone out of style. People who followed mythology prayed, performed rituals, and observed customs much as a modern-day religious person would. One of the oldest of all mythologies, which even had a hand in forming other famous mythologies, is that of Egyptian mythology. Egypt's location in the North of Africa meant that it was in an ideal position to trade with nearby civilizations such as Persia and Greece, and many aspects of their mythologies are echoes of what was picked up in Egypt through trading and discussions.

Egyptian mythology can be traced back to over 5000 years ago, before any mention of Jesus or Muhammed. Tales of Egyptian Gods and Goddesses, monsters, and the interactions they had with each other have been inscribed on pyramid walls, ancient scrolls, and stone pillars that are still marveled at today.

To get a full understanding of Egyptian mythology, it is important to understand the context from which it was formed. This book will delve into what made Ancient Egypt into the powerful civilization that it was. Ancient Egypt was very advanced for its time and made many strides in fields such as engineering, architecture, science, and medicine that are still used in some form today. Such marvels will be discussed in greater detail further on, such as the building of the Pyramids of Giza, the Great Sphinx, and temples of the Valley of Kings. Inventions such as calendars and sundials will show how far ahead some of the advancements in Ancient Egypt really were compared to their counterparts. Some advancements, such as paper, have remained almost identical in modern times.

Mythology, much like modern religion, was used as a way to understand the world around the Ancient Egyptians in a way that their science could not yet explain, as well as to give the people of Ancient Egypt a sense of hope, a sense of justice, and a sense of both what happened before they were born and what will happen to them after they die. But in order to understand how the Ancient Egyptians came to be in this mindset, it is important to understand how they lived. This book will examine the most common jobs and work that Ancient Egyptians performed, their home setting, their family dynamics, their fashion choices, and their entertainment. It will explore both how they saw themselves and how they perceived the world around them. Egypt could only thrive in the way it did thanks to the Nile River, which offered fertile soil in the middle of a hostile desert, and the strong leadership of the Pharaohs which allowed society to grow in size and strength over time. As with any nation, Egypt had its fair shares of war, invasion, and slumps in its development.

These negative times along with the positive times were more easily understandable to Ancient Egyptians if they were the will of the Gods. Fate is far less intimidating than random happenstance. Egypt enjoyed almost 3000 years of prosperity, and such power does not come about by accident. Understandably, Ancient Egyptians attributed this prosperity and success to the will of the Gods and Goddesses that they believed watched over them.

Let this book serve as both a guide and a lens into a world that has long since lost its title as the powerhouse civilization of the world, but has never been forgotten.

Chapter 1: The Might of Egypt

Before the rise of the Mongolian Empire, the Greek Empire, or even the Roman Empire, there was the Egyptian Empire. Egypt was a monument of the Ancient Mediterranean area and even the entire ancient world. The period of time that is considered the great days of Ancient Egypt began at around 3000 BC under the rule of King Narmer of Menes and lasted until the final reign of the famous Cleopatra in 31 AD. This is also what kicked off the Bronze Age as stone tools were being replaced by more intricate and sophisticated bronze tools. In this regard, it can even be stated that Ancient Egypt advanced the world out of the Stone Age. Evidence of farming and settlement in Egypt dates back as far as 5000 BC, so even if ununified and unformed, the birth of Ancient Egyptian Civilization occurred long ago and was an important milestone in human development.

The Pyramids of Giza

As humanity progressed further and developed greater achievements, so too did they begin to develop greater thoughts. These thoughts blossomed into the development of physical structures and creations that we still marvel at and use to this day. One needs to look no further than the Great Pyramids of

Giza, which were constructed between 2550 and 2490 AD in what is still considered to be one of the greatest feats of human engineering. The first and largest was built under the order of Pharaoh Khufu, is around 481 feet tall and built out of approximately 2.3 million stone blocks, with each weighing up to 15 tons. The Second Pyramid was built under the order of Pharaoh Khafre and included in its design was the iconic Sphinx statue. The third and final pyramid was built for Pharaoh Menkaure which, while much smaller, contains the most complex architecture of the three. While the exact construction remains shrouded in mystery, it has been ascertained from records that the builders were both highly skilled and well-fed by the community as it was seen as a national project to highlight the wealth and power of the Pharaohs. The pyramids still stand today as a monument to the power of ancient Egypt and are cited as a major influence on the explosion of growth experienced by Ancient Egypt for millennia to come. The Pyramids themselves serve as a time capsule for life in Ancient Egypt with their depictions of art within their walls of farming, fishing, and rituals to the Gods and Pharaohs. They also provide insight to how Egyptians dressed at the time for Pharaohs, priests, and workers.

Papyrus Paper

One of the most important inventions of Ancient Egypt as well as one of the most important inventions the world has ever known was the invention of paper. Paper was originally made out of the papyrus plant, which gives rise to the origin of the word "paper" itself. The stems of the plants were cut into thin strips, which were then soaked in water and slightly overlaid across each other. This process was repeated, and two sheets would then be laid in a perpendicular fashion across one another. The combined sheet was hammered on a flat surface and then another flat weight was placed on top to allow the sheets to combine as they dried. After a few days of pressure from the two flat surfaces, the paper was removed and smoothed out using a stone. The process was lengthy, but the final product was not very far off from the modern paper we use today. The significance of the invention of paper cannot be overstated as information could now be easily recorded, stored, transported, and taught.

Before the creation of papyrus paper, the written dialect was still found to exist, and the oldest written language ever discovered was ancient Sumerian from 3500 BC, written on the Kish Tablet, a plate of stone. This is believed by scholars to have traveled to Egypt by trade. Although Egyptian hieroglyphics bear no resemblance to Ancient Sumerian, rather, the concept itself is all that was adopted. Ancient Egyptian is the next oldest recorded written language which was also written in stone inside of tombs as far back as 2690 BC. Stone, however, is far more difficult to inscribe upon and lacks the many benefits of recording information that paper provides. The earliest use of the written word is suspected by scholars to be used for trade. It's believed it was used to convey information such as what was for sale and the price of the items. However, there is no evidence of this being its first use. Ancient Egyptian writing officially begins in the way many people instinctively think of Egyptian writing, as hieroglyphics; pictures that describe rather than words that tell.

However, this was only the start of the Egyptian writing journey and the dialect greatly evolved over time by adding logograms, which are symbols representing words, and ideograms, which are symbols representing more obscure thoughts. The direction an image faced was also integral to how it would be read; objects facing each other would interact with each other, and objects facing away from each other were part of a separate thought or used to show leaving or distancing. This also had an impact on whether a line was meant to be read from left to right or from right to left. An example of an ideogram would be a plus sign to show addition. All of this development in writing is owed in no small part to the now more accessible writing and reading medium of papyrus paper.

The Recording of Time

An invention that doesn't even feel like an invention at first glance is the ability to measure time. While the world was a long way away from the invention of a clock, it was still understood in Ancient Egypt that day and night moved in a cycle, and that the cycle could be tracked, at least during the day, by monitoring the movement of the sun. Thus, the first version of the sundial, now referred to as a shadow clock, emerged. The clock contained a round face laid on the ground with a vertical stick that would cast a shadow based on where the sun was in relation to the clock at the time. The most glaring weaknesses of the device being that it only works during the day and with the presence of direct sunlight. The oldest clock dates back to 1500 BC and formed the basis of every clock to come. A less effective but still remarkable clock-like device to measure time at night was also created, known as a Merkht. The Merkht was created around 600 BC and was used to track the alignment of the stars. It suffers a similar weakness to the shadow clock in that it only works with a clear sky.

Another way Ancient Egyptians measured time was with the first calendar. Egypt was a nation that relied heavily on farming as a food source, making it very useful to know which times were good to grow and which times were good to harvest. The earliest calendar dates back to around 3000 BC and records the twelve cycles of the moon which correspond to the twelve months of the year. The calendar was divided into three seasons of four months each, with each month consisting of thirty days. This adds up to a total of 360 days. The seasons coincided with the rise and fall of the Nile River. The first season was called Akhet and was the season of flooding. The second season was Peret and was the season of growth. The third season was the season of Shemu and was the season of harvesting. Egyptians eventually realized they were slightly inaccurate and added in 5 days to compensate for this, resulting in our modern year of 365 days. Owing to a lack of a leap year to make up for the quarter of a day not recorded each year, Egyptians would have a "great year" every three years consisting of 384 days. By 238 BC the calendar was adjusted by invaders such as Ptolemy, and by 25 BC the Alexandrian calendar was introduced.

The Role of Mythology

While there were many other astounding inventions of Ancient Egypt in both the physical and scientific world, there were also the more abstract and philosophical thoughts pondering the Ancient Egyptian minds that are still a part of modern thought. Some of these questions have been answered by modern science such as "how does the sun rise and fall each day?" Others have both scientific and religious variations on their answers such as "where do humans come from?" or "how did the world begin?" and "what happens after we die?" Regardless of how a person may approach these questions today, it remains documented that these questions and more were answered over 5000 years ago through the tales, trials, and tribulations of Egyptian Mythology.

Mythology was used as a way to explain that which could not be explained rationally, such as the power of the sun, the wind, and the Nile. The Nile valley would flood almost annually, which created fertile and arable land in an area surrounded by harsh desert. This led many Ancient Egyptians to pursue a life as a farmer or a fisherman to reap the many treasures the Nile would bestow upon them. Ancient Egypt was essentially an oasis with harshness and death surrounding it. This was certainly considered a miraculous occurrence by its people and so their good fortune was explained by the Gods and Goddesses that make up Egyptian Mythology. These events were not just happenstance for the people of ancient Egypt, they were a gift from the Divine. As thanks for the many gifts bestowed upon them, the Gods would have temples and statues built in their image, their adventures and exploits recorded on temple walls and on papyrus scrolls, they would have rituals to offer up sacrifices of appeasement, and they would have festivals thrown in their honor.

As there were obviously no physical Gods walking among the Ancient Egyptians, the Pharaohs who were the rulers of Ancient Egypt served as the bridge between the Divine world of the Gods, and the physical world in which the Ancient Egyptians resided. The Ancient Egyptians thought of the Gods as kings, and in turn, they also thought of the kings as Gods. This has a large impact on the importance of the souls of the Pharaohs once they departed their mortal coil and transcended towards the afterlife. Mummification, sarcophaguses, and pyramids were considered holy sanctities in allowing the Pharaoh to end their journey on Earth and begin their journey to the afterlife.

Ancient Egypt, like any other civilization both ancient and modern, was at its most powerful and prosperous when it was united. King Narmer (or Menes) understood this and used mythology and its linkage of the different Gods in terms of their lineage, roles, and relevance as a method of unity amongst the different regions of Egypt. In 3000 BC, King Narmer lived in the North of Egypt where the people of the North worshiped Horus. He established his first capital in Thinis, a region of middle Egypt where the people worshipped Osiris. He went on to build a new capital in Memphis, which was located in Southern Egypt, where the people worshipped Ra. Mythology was used as a way to unite these three deities into a sort of holy tribunal linked closely to the Pharaohs to create a connection between Man and Gods to ensure the fertility and prosperity of Egypt.

Chapter 2: Life in Ancient Egypt

Ancient Egypt has managed to preserve itself through its many depictions of not only Gods, monsters, and Pharaohs, but also through depictions of the daily lives of its humbler workers and citizens. Archaeologists have found many relics, paintings, drawings, and scriptures that help modern society paint a picture of a day in the life of the average Ancient Egyptian.

Family and Children

Ancient Egypt put a strong emphasis on the importance of starting a family and of starting a family young. Most marriages were polygamous and featured one husband taking multiple wives. Usually, there would be one wife who was considered the "chief wife" by being the first married or the most senior of the wives. Divorce did exist in Ancient Egypt, but it was very rare as it went against the ideology of a strong family unit. Families were also encouraged to bear multiple children as children were seen as blessings and gifts from the Gods.

Workers

Ancient Egypt was primarily a society built upon agriculture and farming. The majority of male peasants would work in wheat fields while some would become craftsmen such as smiths, tailors, potters, and such. Egyptian farmers were among the earliest civilizations to use oxen to plow the land instead of working entirely with hand plows. Even so, it was a difficult and physically demanding profession. Although there was livestock farming, there was little room for grazing lands, which made meat an expensive commodity only enjoyed by wealthier Egyptians. Fish, when caught, was the primary protein source for most Egyptians. Wheat was the primary food source for most Egyptians and so many would survive on wheat-based products, such as bread, as well as vegetables. Barley was another plentiful grain and, as a result, beer was a very popular drink of Ancient Egypt. There was also wine, but it was primarily reserved for the wealthier members of Egyptian society.

In terms of slave labor, there is controversy and debate. Some scholars believe that slaves in Egypt were paid, albeit meagerly, and functioned more like servants to wealthier Egyptians. This in itself would be considered humiliating for the servants. The same thought goes towards the construction of the pyramids. It is believed the workers were both paid and fed throughout the construction process, however, the job of constructing the pyramids would be a considerably difficult and physically demanding job.

Women

Women were treated almost equally to men in the times of Ancient Egypt. Women were allowed to own their own property as well as their own businesses. Women's testimonies in a court of law were equal to a testimony made by a man. There were even female Pharaohs such as Hatshepsut and Merneith. However, as with most societies of the time, women were seen as caregivers, child rearers, and homemakers. Most Egyptians lived in small houses made from adobe, which is a type of brick made out of mud. Doors and windows were kept shut by hanging mats, which was important for keeping out insects. Some people would live in townhomes, which would be two or three floors tall, with the first floor serving as a business area and the above floors used as living quarters.

Entertainment

Egyptians enjoyed a wide array of entertainment when they weren't working. Egyptians made great use of the Nile River as a source of entertainment through fishing, boat riding, boat racing through rowing, and swimming. Egyptians have also been depicted as competing in athletics for fun, as well as participating in an early version of the sport of hockey. Relics and drawings have been found of children's toys. Some of these toys included wooden carvings of animals, balls, and horses on wheels with strings. Egyptians even had board games. Senet was a popular board game as well as the game Hounds and Jackals, both of which can still be played today but are most likely played with slightly different rules as it is very difficult to determine exactly how these games were played.

Clothing and Fashion

Ancient Egyptians would wear cloth in robe-like fashions which were made from linen. Sandals were the primary footwear and were made from leather and plant materials. Men, women, and children from peasants to royals would all wear makeup. A very popular makeup was called "Kohl" and was worn around a person's eyes. Kohl served as both a cosmetic enhancement as well as for the practical use of protecting the skin from sunburn. Jewelry was also common and popular among all Egyptians of all walks of life. Many would wear rings and amulets as both a sign of fashion as well as religion. Wealthier Egyptians would naturally wear more extravagant jewelry made of more extravagant material such as gold or silver. Small children in artwork were often depicted as not wearing clothes but still wearing jewelry.

Chapter 3: The Egyptian Creation Myth

It has been a burning question on the minds of humanity for millennia and has countless ideas, theories, stories, explanations, and speculations. How did the world begin? This question has been extended further and broader to ask, "how did the universe begin?" as well as being drawn in narrower by asking "how did humans get here?" but it all stems from the same original question. Who or what is "The Creator"?

Scientists and religious figures alike study, ponder, and debate on this topic in the modern era, and five thousand years ago, in Ancient Egypt, it was no different. This is the Egyptian Creation Myth.

Varied Sources

As with any sort of mythological tale, there are certain elements that change slightly depending on who the initial storyteller was. As Ancient Egypt was a superpower of its time, it went through leadership changes, and these changes would often create slight variations to almost all the stories and legends of Egyptian Mythology. The creation myth is no exception; it was used to give more validity towards the current rulers, however, all variations are slight at best and essentially tell the same tale from different perspectives.

These stories were slightly altered, molded, and shaped by the various rulers of Egypt throughout its history, be they Egyptian like Tutankhamun or Ramesses, or foreign invaders such as Nubians or Persians. One of the most influential moments in the history of Ancient Egypt where it is ruled by a foreign body would have to be Alexander the Great, which explains why so many cities have both Greek and Egyptian names recorded in their history. One version of the creation myth states that the world started at the Northern Egypt city of Hermopolis or Megale, depending on if you asked a Greek or Egyptian respectively, and would attribute creation to multiple Gods of chaos. Another version speaks of the ancient city of Heliopolis in more central Egypt, where Atum creates the world. Atum is also sometimes referred to as Anum-Re but is considered the same deity. For simplicity's sake we will refer to this deity as Atum. A third version states the Southern City of Memphis as the site of creation and the God Ptah as the creator.

Of these three major creation stories, the myth recorded within the pyramid text, also known as The Book of the Dead, is that of Heliopolis and Atum. This is the most widely accepted creation myth by modern standards.

Chaos Before Order, Nun

Before the creation of the world, there existed an infinite mass of darkness expanding ever outward. This swirl was described as shapeless and directionless like water; it was known as Nun. The Nun has been personified and given form in the pyramid text as four different couples of men and women. These were the Eight Gods of Chaos, as also mentioned in the Hermopolis version of the creation myth. Each couple served to personify an aspect of Nun. These aspects being the unseen or the invisible Nun, the endless and infinite nature of the water of Nun, the shapeless and formless Nun spreading in all directions, and the immense and complete darkness of Nun.

The God of Gods, Atum-Ra

Out of the chaos of Nun arose Atum, the first God. Atum forced himself out of the dark, shapeless chaos by his own sheer willpower and the power of chanting his own name repeatedly to self-motivate and self-identify in a space that as of yet had no true identity. When Atum arose, it was in the form of a Bennu bird, a bird believed to be a precursor to the mythological phoenix. As a Bennu, he flew to the site where Heliopolis would one day be built. Once there, he approached the Benben, a giant stone obelisk, which he flew into in order to set the Benben alight, thus creating the first sun's rays. These rays pierced the darkness of Nun and began an era of light and creation.

Some other popular sources state that after emerging from the Benben, Atum was henceforth known as Atum-Ra, becoming both the setting sun as Atum and the rising sun as Ra. In other stories, Ra and Atum are almost interchangeable rather than a combined being. This is believed to be due to the efforts of unifying multiple sects of Egyptians to create a more powerful society. This can also be seen in various spelling differences in both Atum and Ra. Atum is referred to at times as Amun and Ra is referred to at times as Re. However, it has been noted that vowels are nowhere to be seen in Ancient Egyptian written text. This could be owing to the fact that written language, in general, was so primitive that it can be attributed to regional dialect. Some scholars have gone as far as to state that Ancient Egypt could almost be considered a monotheistic society rather than a polytheistic society, considering how Ra was held in such high regard above all other Gods.

Atum is depicted as an old human in artwork and is always seen carrying two items. The first item is the ankh, an oval shape with three blunt points protruding to almost create a cross shape; the ankh is a symbol of life. The second item is the *was* scepter, a holy scepter used to depict power and authority as well as royal status. Atum would always be depicted wearing the double crown to represent the unification of upper and lower Egypt. Atum is known as the creator of both Gods and of mankind, as well as the order in the heavens that defeated the chaos.

Ra is similarly depicted holding both an ankh and *was* scepter, however, the most common depictions of Ra feature a human body with a falcon head and a sun disk with a cobra as a headdress. Ra could also be portrayed as a cat and would then go by the name Mau. This is part of the reason why cats were worshiped in Ancient Egypt.

The First Children

The period of Atum coming into existence is known as Zep Temi, which translates to *'the first time'*. it was shortly into Zep Temi that Atum realized that there needed to be more to the world than just himself. So, he used his own being to birth two twin children, a son named Shu and a daughter named Tefnut. He accomplished this feat by spitting them out of his body.

Shu and Tefnut

Shu was the God of wind and of dry air; he represented the essence of what makes life possible for humans. Tefnut was the Goddess of moisture or of wet air, and she represented the passing of time, changing of seasons, and the aging mortality of man. Together, they symbolized what was considered essential principles of humanity: life and truth. Shu and Tefnut went on to separate the sky from the primordial waters of Nun. Tefnut was typically depicted as having a lioness head while Shu has a human head but is depicted as younger than Atum.

At one point, Atum lost Shu and Tefnut within the waters of Nun and removed his own eye to search for them. The Eye found them and helped them to safely return but by then, Atum had replaced his eye with another. The separated eye was furious at being replaced and so to appease it, Atum placed the eye on his forehead to observe the world he was in the process of creating. This eye symbol is known as Udjat.

In creation myths involving Ra instead of Atum, the Eye of Ra is also said to be the creator of the first humans. Upon returning to Ra and seeing itself be replaced, it cried a single teardrop. This teardrop fell to the primitive and barely formed Earth, and out of this drop arose the first humans. This could be considered a major catalyst for Shu and Tefnut to continue their work and create a world for the humans to reside in.

Geb and Nut

Shu and Tefnut became parents of their own twin children. Their children were Geb, the God of earth, and Nut, the Goddess of the sky. Nut was often portrayed as either a cow or an elongated woman stretching over the earth. Geb was the earth that Nut stretched herself over, and the two of them would be divided by their father, Shu.

Geb would lie in a prone position (on his stomach), where plants could grow along his back. He sometimes would also be shown reaching upward towards Nut with his outstretched arm forming mountains. The ocean or the Nile River would also be shown on Geb's back, flowing from one side to the other to create fertile land in which to grow and prosper. The rest of his back would be shown as red desert, harsh and barren and devoid of life. The desert would continue into the underworld depicted underneath Geb. Geb was sometimes referred to as a sort of cosmic goose that had laid the egg of the universe, as he was the source of all the land on Earth as the Egyptians knew it.

Nut, as Goddess of the sky, was also responsible for ensuring the rising sun each morning, which has sometimes been depicted as a scarab beetle rolling the sun as if it were a pile of dung, while being overseen by Nut. Another explanation of the sun's rise and fall is given in the form of Ra and his boat, which would sail across the heavens carrying the sun. The boat was known as "The Barque of Millions of Years." The boat would begin its journey in the East to raise the sun and was referred to as Madjet, which translates to "strengthening." As the boat began to lower in the West it was referred to as Semektet, which translates to "weakening." Once Semektet was weak enough it would be devoured by Nut; this gave Nut the association as the Protector of the dead. Ra would then begin a journey into the underworld, essentially dying to be reborn the next day. This further strengthens the notion that the Bennu bird is an early influence on the phoenix.

The Five Gods of Creation

While some of the details change in certain places between stories, these five beings are considered to be the foundation of the physical and metaphysical realm for the Ancient Egyptians. Atum-Ra is thought to be the most important God in all of Egyptian Mythology and would go on to receive the most temples, statues, and sacrifices in his honor. The children and grandchildren of Atum-Ra would create the world as we know it, but would, in turn, give thanks to the parent who brought them into being.

Chapter 4: Egyptian Gods and Goddesses

Up until now, we have only spoken about the Gods and Goddesses that were directly involved with the Creation Myth. Within the creation Myth, the story spans three generations from Amun down until Geb and Nut. From this point onwards the other Gods and Goddesses are the continuation of this lineage. Geb and Nut went on to produce four children, all of which also serve very important roles in Egyptian Mythology. These four children are considered four of the principal deities of Zep Temi. They are Osiris, Set, Isis, and Nephthys.

Osiris

Osiris was the firstborn child of Geb and Nut, making him first in line to inherit the throne of Egypt. He is the Egyptian God of the dead, the underworld, and the afterlife. Osiris was often depicted as a human male with green or black skin as well as a beard. Green was a color associated with rebirth, and black was a color associated with fertility, as it is the color of rich and fertile soil. He wore a crown that had two ostrich feathers and occasionally included the moon into its design. His legs would be wrapped in bandages like a mummy. It was believed that all of the dead kings would reside with Osiris and at some point, they would all be resurrected together from the afterlife as long as they performed the appropriate rituals, such as mummification. In his hands, he would hold a flail and a crook, which is a rod with a crooked top piece. These two items were symbolic of the leadership of the harvest, with the flail representing the fertility of a toiled land and the crook representing the authority of the shepherd, earning him his other title of the Shepherd God.

Although being heavily associated with death, he was considered to be a very merciful and just ruler of the afterlife. Osiris is also credited as being responsible for the flooding of the Nile. For this reason, he is also seen as responsible for granting life as well as being responsible for the afterlife and eventually the resurrection from the afterlife. Although Osiris is the name he is most famously associated with, it is a name of Latin origin, and his Egyptian name was Wsjr, believed to be pronounced as Aser, User, or Weser. Other lesser-used titles of Osiris include The Lord of Silence, The Lord of Love, and The Eternally Youthful Lord.

Isis

Isis was the Mother Goddess, though she was also the Goddess of fertility, marriage, medicine, and magic. Isis became the Goddess of magic through tricking the now much older God, Ra. She collected the saliva of Ra that would sometimes trickle from his mouth. This saliva was mixed with the earth to create a mighty snake which then bit Ra. Isis, being the Goddess of medicine, promised to heal Ra if he would tell her his true sacred name, the name which he used to will himself into existence. Ra succumbed and told her his secret name which not only granted her power over Ra, but opened her to many new magical abilities.

Isis was often depicted as a human woman wearing a vulture headdress. The vulture would often appear to sit on her head facing forward with its wings coming down on either side behind her ears. Sometimes, Isis would wear a double crown with ram horns surrounding a sun disc. She would wear a jeweled collar and a dress that stretched to the ground. She would hold a papyrus scepter and an ankh, the symbol of life.

Isis was known by many other names, which in turn held many other titles, some of which include:

- Usert: The Earth Goddess
- Ankhet: The Fertility God of the Waters
- Tcheft: Goddess overseeing the sacrifices humans made to Gods
- Satis: Goddess with the power of the Nile
- Khut: Goddess of the New Year and new beginnings
- Thenenet: Goddess of the afterlife
- Renenet: Goddess of the harvest

Isis was depicted as being a woman with great power, intelligence, and influence, which earned her the unofficial title of the ideal mother. She was an immensely popular Goddess, especially amongst women, and she developed a cult following throughout Egypt, even spreading into parts of Europe. Isis was often depicted nursing her child Horus, or even nursing the Pharaohs. Some scholars believe that the stories of Isis had an influence on the stories of the Virgin Mary.

Set

Set was the second born son of Geb and Nut. he was known as the God of chaos, and darkness. Set has a rather unique depiction when compared to other Gods. He is shown to have a human male body and the head of an animal, however, the animal is not as recognizable as the falcon of Ra or the lioness of Tefnut. The animal is simply referred to as the Set animal. It had a long-pointed snout, and upward-facing elongated ears with rectangular edges. When the Set animal was portrayed with a body, it had a dog-like shape with a forked tail. Set would be shown holding an ankh in one hand and a *was* staff in the other. The *was* staff had the head of the Set animal carved into the end. Set was associated with many other animals including the boar, antelope, crocodile, snake, scorpion, and hippopotamus.

Set was also known as God of drought and the desert, therefore responsible for the lack of growth and fertility when compared to his siblings Isis and Osiris. Sometimes also referred to as the God of storms and the God of war, he was an ideal placeholder God for anything the Egyptians saw as evil, dangerous, or unwanted. Set was associated with the color red, which was the worst color to ancient Egyptians, who reviled people with red skin and animals with red fur. Set had loyal followers but also had many who opposed the worship of such a being, and as a result, his statues and temples were at times destroyed by priests who did not worship him.

Although Set is often seen as an evil and wicked God, he was well-respected by the Pharaohs. There were even some Pharaohs, such as Pharaoh Seti I, who were directly named after the God of chaos. Set was seen as one of two Gods, the other being Horus, who bestowed power and leadership onto the Pharaohs. Set was seen as a duality or opposing force towards the other Gods rather than a directly villainous being. They believed that light and good cannot exist without darkness and evil, respectively. Therefore, in order to have heroic Gods performing heroic acts, they needed the opposition of Set.

Nephthys

Nephthys was the second born daughter of Geb and Nut. Of the four children, she is by far the least documented and as a result, the least is known about her. Some scholars speculate that she was only introduced to be a counterpart to Isis in the same sense that Set is the counterpart to Osiris, as her only major role in

Egyptian Mythology appears to be the story of Isis and Osiris. Nephthys was seen as the embodiment of death, decay, and darkness. However, as is often the case with death in Egyptian mythology, she is also seen as a Goddess of air, regeneration, rebirth, virility, life after death, and was shown to have great healing powers. Appearance-wise, Nephthys is very similar to Isis and can often only be distinguished by a different headdress, which was usually a basket on her head.

With the four children of Geb and Nut established, it is fair to say that none of them are truly understood until we dive into the story of Isis and Osiris.

The Myth of Isis and Osiris

Once the four children were born, they became betrothed to one another. Osiris was married to Isis and Set was married to Nephthys. Osiris was the next ruler of Egypt, a position Set envied, and it is also said that Set lusted after Isis more so than he did for Nephthys. Osiris decided that he wanted to travel across the world (the world being Egypt) to bring civilization to its people. In his absence from the throne, he named his wife Isis the Queen Regent of Egypt. Set felt as though he should have been named Regent in his brother's absence as his jealousy only grew greater.

Set decided to take matters into his own hands and invited his brother Osiris to a banquet to be held in his honor. Osiris, having no mutual feelings of grievance towards his brother Set, happily agreed to attend. Set had created a large and beautiful chest made of cedarwood and ebony, which was placed as the centerpiece of entertainment at the banquet. He used it as a sort of contest in which he promised to gift the chest to any of his guests who could fit into it. This was a trap as he had the chest designed so that only Osiris would fit. Osiris joined in on the festivities with all the other guests and climbed into the chest, only to find that it was a perfect fit for his body, and he was awarded the chest by Set. Unfortunately for Osiris, this is exactly where Set wanted him. While he was still inside the chest, Set closed the lid and nailed it shut. Set then proceeded to seal the chest using molten lead and threw what was now to be the coffin of Osiris into the Nile River.

The chest was carried out into the ocean and washed up on the shores of Byblos, which is close to modern-day Lebanon. As the coffin made contact with the shoreline, a gigantic tree sprouted, known as the Tamarisk tree, in order to protect Osiris. The legend states that the tree was so large that the King of Byblos desired it for his palace, so he cut the tree down and made it into a mighty pillar. This resulted in the King of Byblos possessing the deceased body of Osiris.

The now widowed Isis was utterly heartbroken to find out the news of the death of her husband and sought out his body. She tracked Osiris to Byblos and found that the King had taken Osiris as his personal trophy. The King had a child who was bitten by a dangerous snake, and upon learning this, Isis offered the King a trade. She would cure the child with her powers of medicine in exchange for the body of Osiris. The King agreed to this trade. Osiris was brought back to Egypt where Isis was able to revive him for long enough that they could conceive a child together and name him Horus, although in some versions of the story Isis was already pregnant with Horus before Osiris died. Not long after, when the dead body of Osiris was left unattended by Isis while tending to Horus, Set struck again.

Set cut the body of Osiris into fourteen pieces and hid the pieces all across Egypt. In some versions of the story there were sixteen pieces. Isis once again found herself mortified by the actions of her brother, so she formed an alliance with her sister and wife of Set, Nephthys, to help her track down the missing pieces of her husband.

Nephthys had a son of her own named Anubis. There are varied accounts on whether Anubis was the son of Set or the son of Osiris. As Set would lust for Isis, so too would Nephthys lust for Osiris. Nephthys, on at least one occasion, disguised herself as Isis and seduced Osiris.

Isis and Nephthys ventured across all of Egypt and found all of the body parts, except one. It is said that Set specifically fed that part to a sacred fish. Isis and Nephthys mourned over the remaining pieces of their lost brother and lover. Ra took notice of this and gave instructions to Isis, Nephthys, and Thoth (the God of Knowledge and representative of Ra) on how to put the pieces back together to form a mostly whole body. Ra then sent Anubis to perform the first-ever mummification on the newly reformed body of Osiris. Isis transformed herself into a small bird called a kite and breathed one final breath of life into Osiris to say goodbye before he departed into the underworld, where he would become its ruler. Ra assured Osiris that he would find peace in the underworld as its king and that his son Horus would one day take his place as the rightful King of Egypt.

Anubis

Anubis is considered by many to be the most iconic God in all of Egyptian Mythology. Anubis is his Greek name, and his Egyptian name was either Inpu or Anpu. As previously stated, his exact parentage is debated between Nephthys and Set or Nephthys and Osiris. He was depicted as a human male with the head of a jackal. Jackals and wild dogs would often be found on the outskirts of villages, which is mostly where the cemeteries were constructed. He would often be portrayed in black, a color associated with growth and rebirth. He would mostly be portrayed holding an ankh, to symbolize life, and a flail or a staff.

He was the original God of the underworld until Osiris joined him in the underworld and was given the title by Anubis out of respect. Anubis still served a very important role in the embalming, funeral, and eventual judgement of the dead. Priests would wear jackal-headed masks of Anubis during the mummification process. Part of the preparation of the dead included the use of sweet-smelling herbs, as these were believed to attract Anubis to the body and help him to guide the pure of heart into paradise. The judgement of Anubis on whether a person was pure or not was a simple test. Anubis would have a scale and on one end of the scale rested a single feather, representing the principle of "Ma'at" or "truth." On the other end, Anubis would place the heart of the deceased. If the heart was not weighed down by the sins of its life, it would be lighter than the feather and would tip upwards. If the heart was burdened by sin it would be heavier than the feather and tip downwards. This would decide their fate in the afterlife and was the reason Anubis held the title of "Guardian of the Scales." Anubis also famously defeated enemies of Egypt known as the Nine Bows to grant him the title of "Jackal Ruler of Bows." Anubis had a wife named Anput, who also had a jackal's head, and together they had a daughter named Kebechet who is the Goddess of Purification.

Horus

Horus is considered to be the first national God of Egypt, in the sense that the entire nation of Egypt recognized his authority. The actual name Horus means "The one from above" indicating his status above other Gods. Horus is always depicted as having a falcon head, and so over time several other Gods that had connections to falcons became Horus and combined into the Horus mythos. Horus is often depicted holding a scepter and an ankh like many of the other powerful Gods. He would wear a white and red crown that symbolized the unity of all of Egypt. Some of his titles include: Sun God, God of War, God of Dawn, Keeper of Wisdom, Ruler of Two Lands, and God of Kings. Horus was seen as the patron saint of the current Pharaoh, which gave any current Pharaoh the title of "Living Horus." Horus would rest as a falcon on the shoulder of the Pharaoh until the Pharaoh died and went over to Osiris. The Horus would protect the next Pharaoh and rest on their shoulder, too.

In the most ancient versions of Egyptian Mythology, Horus was the son of Ra. He held domain over both the sun and the moon, which represented the two eyes of Horus, who ruled over both day and night. Horus and Ra were combined into a singular God on many occasions. There are also some stories which place Horus as a brother of Osiris and Set rather than a son or nephew, respectively. One explanation of this version of the story speaks of Osiris impregnating Isis with Horus while still in the womb. The most popular current version of the history of Horus is that of the Isis and Osiris myth mentioned earlier, in which he is conceived after the revival of Osiris.

Continuing the Myth of Isis and Osiris

As a child, Horus was kept protected and sheltered from the world by his mother, Isis. There are many artworks depicting Isis caring for young Horus and he is often pictured on a lotus leaf. As Horus grew into a young man, he was slowly becoming a favorite of the other Gods. This greatly angered his uncle and current ruler of Egypt, Set. Horus and Set fought in many great battles, but Horus eventually triumphed over his uncle and took his place at the throne of Egypt.

One of the most famous of these battles involved both Horus and Set transforming into hippos and fighting in the Nile River. From this story, a tradition grew in which the Pharaoh would battle a hippo in the Nile armed with only a spear, as this was symbolic of the might of the Pharaoh that had the favor of Horus.

Another famous battle between Horus and Set involves Set defeating Horus and damaging his left eye in the process. Horus's left eye was known as the moon eye, and as a result of this injury, we have the different phases of the moon. The God Thoth was able to heal the eye, and from this story, the Eye of Horus was born. The Eye of Horus, also known as the Wedjat Eye, is one of the most famous symbols in all of Egyptian Mythology and features an eyeball with a curved tail and a teardrop forming on the right side. The eye was believed to watch over the world and protect it from chaos. Famous depictions of the eye have been found on boats for protection during travel and were even found on the Mummy of King Tutankhamen.

Thoth

Thoth is the God of Magic, Knowledge, and Writing. Some sources credit him as being born from Ra/Horus and others as born of Set. This duality of origins has resulted in Thoth being seen as a source of neutrality, equilibrium, and balance. Thoth's Egyptian name was Djehuty, meaning "he who is like an ibis" and is depicted as a human male with the head of an ibis, a long-beaked bird. The ibis was a sacred bird in Ancient Egypt and was associated with wisdom; it was also a popular pet. Thoth's greatest role in Egyptian Mythology is that of the scribe who would record events as they occurred and would often offer advice to other Gods. Thoth has been depicted as healing both Horus and Set during their many battles, offering no favoritism.

This resulted in Thoth being seen as a source of fairness and justice. Thoth is considered in Egyptian Mythology to be the father of law, science, magic, philosophy, and writing. Thoth has been credited with giving the gift of writing to humans. It is said that scribes would pour out one drop of ink in Thoth's honor before writing.

Thoth appears in versions of the Creation Myth as well. When Nut became pregnant, Ra was furious and forbade her from giving birth on any day of the year. Thoth made a bet with Khonsu, God of the Moon, over a game of Senet and gambled five days of moonlight. Thoth was victorious and converted the five nights into five days that did not previously exist in the year, and was therefore not affected by Ra's decree. In these five new days, Nut gave birth to her five children (including Horus in this version). Ra was impressed that Thoth had found a loophole to his order and offered him a seat of honor in Ra's boat, which crossed the heaven each day and night.

Thoth was married to Seshat, although sometimes she was portrayed as his daughter. She is also a Goddess of Wisdom and is heavily associated with the library of the Gods and working as a scribe of the Pharaohs.

Thoth was also involved in the proceedings of the rituals of the dead alongside Osiris and Anubis. Thoth would record the results of the weighing. He had a palace in the afterlife known as the Mansion of Thoth. The Mansion was a sanctuary that souls could stop at to rest, as well as a school to learn magic to defeat demons on the road to paradise. There was a belief that Thoth had inscribed all of his knowledge into sacred books of magic that were hidden for a later generation to find, though no such books have ever been found.

These are some of the most popular and worshipped Gods and Goddesses in Egyptian Mythology, however, there are many more minor Gods. It is also worth noting that different Gods and Goddesses of smaller status have had their stories woven into the tapestry of one of these greater and more powerful deities. This is often the reason for different sources claiming different titles, roles, and sometimes even family trees for the Egyptian Gods and Goddesses. Scholars speculate that smaller sects of Egyptians would have the Gods that they believed in combined with larger Gods in order to make assimilation into a more united Egyptian society possible. If it was still your God, just with another name and a slightly altered story, it was still far easier to accept than a new God entirely.

Ma'at

Ma'at is a fairly unique, but very important facet in the realm of Egyptian Mythology. Ma'at was shown to be a physical Goddess but can be better understood as a personification of an ideology rather than a more physical presence like the previous Gods that have been discussed. Ma'at can be directly translated to mean "being straight," but has also been used to exemplify the principles of truth, order, justice, and balance. Ma'at is thought to have been formed when Ra first arose from the waters of Nun and is therefore sometimes considered a daughter to Ra. She is also sometimes considered to be the wife of Thoth as they both have ties to order and justice. Ma'at would also accompany both Thoth and Ra on his boat trips across the heavens. Some of the other titles of Ma'at include the Eye of Ra, the Lady of the Underworld, and the Mistress of the Heavens.

Ma'at was seen as the principle that held order. Ma'at was the reason why the sun and moon would rise and set, why the Nile would flood, and why the stars would return to their same positions in the night sky. Egyptians were expected to uphold Ma'at and protect her in their daily lives, and the Pharaoh was seen as the guardian of Ma'at in the realm of man. If Ma'at were ever to fall, the waters of Nun would plunge the world back into a shapeless, formless, infinite darkness once again.

In order to incorporate Ma'at into their daily lives, she was made an important part of the legal system. Ma'at was thought of as being responsible for human relationships and human behavior. The priests of Ma'at would operate as a panel of judges as they had the best understanding of Ma'at. There are many artworks of Pharaohs holding a statue of Ma'at when swearing to uphold truth and justice, in the same way a person would swear on a bible in a modern court.

Ma'at was portrayed as a slim human female thought to represent the perfect Egyptian woman. She wore a crown with a single ostrich feather. This was the feather that was used in the afterlife on the scale to weigh a person's heart, as the feather of Ma'at is also a feather of truth and justice. She was also shown in artwork, like many other Gods, to hold an ankh and a scepter. Ma'at was occasionally portrayed to have wings. She was often represented as a stone platform to show the strength and stability of the order emerging from the chaotic waters of Nun.

Sobek

Sobek was the Egyptian God of Strength, Power, and the Nile River. He was portrayed as a human male with a crocodile head. He wore an elaborate crown that featured two large horns, a sun disc, and snakes. His other titles included "Lord of the Waters" for his association with the Nile River, and "The Rager" as he was often portrayed to be violent and temperamental. He was often depicted with the ankh and scepter.

Ancient Egyptians had mixed relationships with the crocodile. They feared them as they were threatening predators that lived along the Nile River, but they also loved them and saw them as a symbol of great power. Crocodiles were also thought to represent fertility due to their sheer numbers. Sobek was thought to offer strength to the Egyptian armies and the Pharaohs to allow them to slay their enemies and protect the nation of Egypt. Crocodiles were kept in temples and had pools dedicated to them. They would be given jewelry and fed well. There are even mummified crocodiles that have been found ranging from eggs to fetuses to full-grown adults.

Sobek was believed to be the son of Set and Neith, who was a Goddess of War. This further connected him to his military responsibilities. He was considered, much like a real crocodile, to be fierce, powerful, erratic, and unpredictable, all positive characteristics in war. He was also considered to be overly sexual with women due to his ties to fertility. He did take a wife named Renenutet, who was the Goddess of Plenty and was thought of as a symbol of luck and good fortune for Egyptians. She was known as the Cobra Goddess, and like Sobek, could be seen as very threatening to enemies and very strong to allies. Snakes would often be found amongst the wheat fields, but they would eat the mice and other pests that threatened the harvest, therefore offering a plentiful harvest and good fortune. She was depicted as a human woman with the head of a cobra which also featured two horns and a sun disc. Together, they had a son named Khonsu, who became the God of the Moon and Time.

Chapter 5: Egyptian Monsters and Other Stories

Egyptian Mythology is full of many powerful Gods and Goddesses who performed amazing feats. Some of these were in the form of great battles, where both physical and mental abilities of these Gods were tested. Set has already been named as a God who would clash with other Gods, but there were other creatures of great power and strength who, while not Gods in the sense that they were worshipped, still possessed amazing characteristics to sometimes even rival that of the Gods. These are the monsters of Ancient Egypt.

Ammit

Known primarily as Ammit the Devourer, Ammit was a female monster who resided in the underworld. Ammit was depicted as having the head of a crocodile, the torso of a lion, and the legs of a hippo. All of these animals were considered to be dangerous and powerful to Egyptians. When an Egyptian was being judged in the underworld, they would have to use the scale of Anubis to weigh their heart against the feather of Ma'at. If they lived a life of truth and righteousness, then their heart would weigh less than the feather and they would be granted passage into heaven. However, if their heart was weighed down by sins and weighed more than the feather, then their soul would be fed to Ammit, the devourer of souls. Once a soul was swallowed by Ammit, it was said to be restless and in pain forever, to die a second death. Ammit was seen as the final fate of the wicked.

Apep

Apep, also known as Apophis, was a gigantic snake monster most commonly noted as being an enemy to Ra. Apep was often depicted as a coiled serpent in order to help convey his massive size, and in many artworks is seen directly in battle with the Gods or alternatively, dismembered and being defeated by the Gods. Every day, Ra would sail his barge across the heavens to facilitate the rise and fall of the sun, and every day this became the battleground between Ra and Apep, who sought to destroy the cycle of the sun by destroying Ra. Egyptian priests would give many blessings and perform many rituals in the name of Ra in order to ensure that Ra could defeat Apep every day. Apep is seen as a vessel of chaos who wished to return the world to the chaos of Nun. Apep was thought to be responsible for earthquakes, storms, and thunder. Apep has been linked to the God Set as a servant, but there have also been depictions of Set doing battle with Apep. One of the most famous depictions of Apep is his defeat to Mau, a great cat who was the personification of Ra.

Griffin

Griffins are powerful bird-like creatures with the head, wings, and front talons of an eagle, as well as the body, hind legs, and tail of a lion. Both of these animals are considered amongst the most powerful of predators and so the griffin is considered a very powerful monster. Griffins have appeared in multiple different mythologies ranging from Medieval, to Persian, to Greek, but their origins can be traced back to Ancient Egypt over 4000 years ago. Griffins are often associated with military might and have been featured on many shields and armor plates.

El Naddaha

El Naddaha is quite a unique case in terms of monsters of Egyptian Mythology, as she is actually a relatively recent addition to the pantheon. The story can be traced to as recently as the 20th century but is in no way less of a myth than any other monster. El Naddaha was a beautiful woman with an equally beautiful voice who would wander along the banks of the Nile River. Egyptian men would hear her beautiful voice calling them by their names and would want to get closer to this mysterious and beautiful woman. Once they were alone, the men would be drowned in the Nile. El Naddaha is also believed to be inspired by sirens of Greek Mythology and djinns of Muslim Mythology.

Sphinx

Sphinxes, much like griffins, have featured in multiple mythologies over multiple centuries, most notably in Greece and Turkey. However, none can argue that the most famous Sphinx of all is the Great Sphinx of Egypt, whose architecture is marveled alongside the pyramids. The depiction of the sphinx in Greek and Turkish tales is somewhat different from the Egyptian portrayal. In the Greek and Turkish tales, the sphinx has the head of a woman on the body of a lioness, which may or may not have eagle wings. These sphinxes were depicted as malevolent, cunning, and ruthless. The Egyptian sphinx has the head of a man on a lion's body and has a far calmer and neutral demeanor. The human-headed sphinx is also referred to as an androsphinx. Less famous versions of Egyptian sphinxes included the criosphinx, which had the head of a ram, and the hieracosphinx, which had the head of a falcon. Sphinxes in all cultures were considered to be mighty creatures who made ideal guardians for various temples and tombs. The sphinx mythology often includes a variant of answering a riddle, but this is mostly tied with the Greek version of the sphinx.

Uraeus

Uraeus was another mystical snake of Egyptian Mythology. Uraeus is believed to have been created by Isis out of dust. Always depicted as an upright cobra, Uraeus has the title of "The Risen One." Uraeus has been used as a symbol of authority, divinity, and royalty. As such, it is donned on many headdresses of both Gods and Pharaohs. The symbol of Uraeus was meant to represent that the wearer had the favor of Wadjet, an old Goddess worshipped in Lower Egypt. As Uraeus represented Lower Egypt, a vulture was a symbol of Upper Egypt, showing protection from Nekhbet, an older Goddess of Upper Egypt. These two animals were often donned together on crowns and headdresses to symbolize a united Egypt.

From these monsters as well as many of the backgrounds and origins of the aforementioned Gods, it can be seen how large an impact Egyptian Mythology has had on other countries. Greece, Rome, Persia, and even Christianity can trace many roots back to the sands of Ancient Egypt. While the creation myth and the myth of Isis and Osiris may be amongst the most well-known and well-documented tales of Egyptian Mythology, there is no shortage of other famous stories that have survived for thousands of years, some of which have even been modernized and may sound familiar.

The Girl with the Red Slippers

There was once a slave girl known as Rhapdosis. Rhapdosis worked in a grand mansion located in Memphis near the Nile River where there were many other slaves, but they would not speak to her. The slave girls refused to speak to her because they were jealous of her beauty, and the slave boys would not speak to her because they thought her beauty made her arrogant and snobbish. This was not the case, as Rhapdosis was a very gentle and sweet person, although she was very shy. She was not born a slave; she was captured when she was very young. She only had one possession from her life before she became a slave, a pair of beautiful red slippers.

Rhapdosis treasured these slippers and would never wear them, especially around the other slaves. She would keep them hidden in her quarters. Sometimes, when she was alone, Rhapdosis would fetch her slippers and hold them up to the sun or moon, whether it was day or night, and watch as the stones glistened in the light. She knew that the stones were fake jewelry, but still found the slippers to be beautiful and comforting.

One night, when all the slaves were asleep, Rhapdosis grabbed her slippers and climbed up onto the rooftop. Rhapdosis was exhausted from a very long day at work and really needed the comfort of her slippers glistening in the moonlight. Suddenly, an eagle swooped down from out of the air and grabbed one of the slippers, carrying it off into the night sky. Rhapdosis was heartbroken.

In the city of Thebes, the Pharaoh was relaxing in his royal garden with his Vizier. The Vizier was recounting the Pharaoh with all the matters of the day, as he did every night. The eagle flew into the garden and dropped the slipper directly into the Pharaoh's lap. The Pharaoh was initially very shocked and then became very impressed with the great beauty of the slipper. The Vizier told the Pharaoh that the slipper must belong to a very wealthy woman and that he would see if any city has reported a missing bejeweled slipper.

Four days later, the Vizier received news that the missing slipper had been reported in the city of Memphis and that the person reporting it was a slave girl. The Vizier was very shocked and couldn't believe a slave could own such a beautiful treasure. They traveled to Memphis personally to inspect the situation, where he found Rhapdosis and asked for proof that she was the owner. She went to her hiding spot and removed the other slipper.

The Vizier was amazed. He said to Raphdosis, "the eagle that brought your slipper to the Pharaoh was a sign from Horus. You must come with me to meet the Pharaoh." The Vizier gave the slave owners a gold bracelet in exchange for her freedom and they departed Memphis together. The Pharaoh and Rhapdosis met, fell in love, and lived happily ever after. Can you see what modern-day fairytale this story might have influenced?

The Princess of Bekhten

The Pharaoh was on a journey to lands in the North of Egypt, collecting tributes from nearby kingdoms, including the land of Bekhten. Most of the chiefs offered up the usual assortment of treasures as a tribute to the Pharaoh, such as gold and jewels, but the Prince of Bekhten offered to the Pharaoh his eldest daughter. The Pharaoh found her to be very beautiful and accepted the offer. He made her his chief royal wife and gave her the name "Ra-Neferu" which means "The beauties of Ra."

A few years later, the Prince of Bekhten traveled to Thebes to meet with the Pharaoh. He was visiting to inform the Pharaoh that Ra-Neferu's younger sister, Bent-Reshet, had become very sick and implored the help of the Pharaoh's team of medical physicians. The Pharaoh agreed and gathered his greatest medical minds, asking them to choose one of them to return to Bekhten with the Prince to aid Bent-Reshet. The royal scribe

Tehuti-Em-Beb was chosen and made the journey up North with the Prince. He examined her and found that her disease was not a disease at all, but possession by an evil spirit that he was not strong enough to exorcise. He told the Prince that only a God could vanquish this spirit.

The Pharaoh was told by an Envoy of what had transpired and personally set out for the Temple of Khonsu, a powerful God of the Moon and Time. he prayed to Khonsu for help in removing the evil trapped within the Princess of Bekhten. Khonsu took residence in a statue in the Temple and instructed the Pharaoh to send the statue to Bekhten.

The statue arrived and Khonsu confronted the demon, defeating him easily, and removing him from the Princess. The demon apologized and asked if he could partake in a meal with Khonsu before returning to the spirit world. A great feast was held for Khonsu and the spirit, after which the spirit left as promised. The Prince realized the power of Khonsu and decided to keep his statue for himself. Khonsu remained in Bekhten for three years, until he decided to return to Egypt and took the form of a gold hawk to fly back. The Prince felt ashamed for keeping Khonsu for so long and sent many offerings back to Egypt to appease the God. The Pharaoh had all of these treasures placed in the Temple of Khonsu.

Chapter 6: Temples of the Gods

While the stories of the Egyptian Gods and Goddesses captivated and shaped the minds of the Egyptian people, they were still only stories with no physical presence. To the Egyptian people, religion was a tremendous part of their culture, and in order to have the Gods and Goddesses feature in their religion of the Earthly plane, they would need a physical representation. The Pharaohs were considered to be conduits of the Gods but there needed to be something more accessible to the average Egyptian. This role was fulfilled by temples.

Temples were beacons of social gatherings and also held great political power based on who was being worshipped in the temple. Temples owned their own land, and often also owned farmland that would provide its priests with food. Aside from priests, other people were also employed by the temple including craftsmen, cleaners, and farmers. Temples were also gifted spoils of war by Pharaohs.

Types of Temples

Temples of Ancient Egypt served two functions, worshipping and funeral proceedings of the Pharaohs. A religious temple would often feature multiple Gods within its halls, but there would be one main God to whom the site was dedicated. Priests would offer sacrifices, perform rituals, conduct ceremonies, and pray to the Gods. When a Pharaoh would die, the funeral cult of priests would dress and prepare the body for the journey into the afterlife. A mortuary temple would be specifically built for a specific Pharaoh and as such, could sometimes reflect the life of the Pharaoh as much as their death. Some mortuary temples were built as extensions or nearby to the Pharaoh's tomb. Some Pharaohs chose to hide their tombs and therefore ordered their mortuary temples to be built at a separate location.

Famous Temples

Not all temples were created equally. As previously stated, a temple could be seen as a symbol of political power and be used by a Pharaoh as a display of might and unity of Egypt. The most famous collection of temples was located to the west of the Nile River, known as The Theban Necropolis. The word "Necropolis" can be translated to mean "City of the Dead."

Hatshepsut's Mortuary Temple

Hatshepsut was a female Pharaoh in approximately 1470 BC. Her Temple stands at the front of The Valley of Kings. The temple is known as "Djeser Djeseru" which means "Holy of Holiest." The temple took 15 years to construct, stood at 97 feet tall, and had three levels. Leading up through all three levels was a 100-foot long causeway that was believed to have sphinxes and exotic trees on either side. The first level's main feature was a colonnade, which is a large room with pillars that depicted her numerous journeys to the city of Punt. However, today many of these have been destroyed. The second level had another colonnade with similar depictions. These are considered to be the oldest recorded proof of a trade expedition. There is a shrine dedicated to Anubis, as well as another shrine dedicated to Hathor, the Goddess of funerals. There are also artworks depicting Hatshepsut as being the daughter of Ra. The third level has statues of Horus and a portico, which is a sort of external room supported by columns, and these columns were shaped like Hatshepsut. Behind the portico was a courtyard that led to many chambers. Large portions of the temple were destroyed by future Pharaohs who did not approve of Hatshepsut. Many sections of the temple were reconstructed by Egyptologists in the 20th century.

The Ramesseum

King Ramesses II had a temple built known as The Ramesseum, and it was constructed over 20 years during his 67-year reign from 1279-1213 BC. It has been less well preserved than Hatshepsut's temple and has been damaged by flooding from the Nile River. The temple was 600 feet long and 220 feet wide. Inside the temple was a 57-foot tall statue of Ramesses II, and at the base of the statue these words are inscribed: "My name is Ozymandias, King of Kings: Look upon my works, ye Mighty, and despair." There are also many smaller statues of the Pharaoh. The temple is decorated with many artworks depicting the many military victories of King Ramesses II. The center of the temple is known as Hypostyle Hall which is held up by 29 columns. There are two rows of Osiris columns in the second courtyard which are still well preserved, however, the first courtyard has been severely damaged over time. To the west of the temple, there was a library, a linen room, a shrine dedicated to Ra, as well as a small mud temple where Ramesses II would rest during the construction of his temple. The Ramessuem also houses one of the earliest arches in recorded history, a true marvel of architecture for the time. There are also two smaller temples built near his temple, one for his first wife, and one for his mother.

Medinet Habu

Ramesses III was Pharaoh from 1186 until 1155 BC. He was considered to be the last great Pharaoh and his temple known as Medinet Habu reflected this. His temple spread across over 75,000 feet and even enclosed Hatshepsut's temple within his own temple. Egyptians have regarded Medinet Habu as sacred and magical ground ever since its foundation, and as recently as 1977 when Libya invaded Egypt it was believed to protect the Egyptian people. Many festivals honoring Amun were held at Medinet Habu.

The entrance to the temple was modeled after a Syrian fortress, which Ramesses III had observed during his military campaigns, and was known as the Migdol Gate. At the Migdol gate are also two large statues of Sekhmet, who was a warrior Goddess. To the right of the Migdol Gate is Hatshepsut's temple, while on the left of the Gate are the Chapels of Votaresses, which were built well after the death of Ramesses III, in around 700 BC.

The Votaresses were high priestesses of Amun in Thebes who also served as governors. There is a large Ptolemaic Pylon to the South East, and it is decorated with a large sun disc as well as depictions of the many victories in battle Egypt amassed under the leadership of King Ramesses III. There is a sacred lake in the southeast corner where women would come to clean themselves and pray for their children.

Behind the Pylon is a court surrounded by columns. The columns are decorated with artwork of Ramesses III being adored by many queens that are smaller than he is. To the left was the Royal Palace which featured a window known as the Window of Appearances. This window was used by Ramesses III to award his commanding officers with golden collars for their war efforts. There is a second Pylon that features the artwork of Ramesses III delivering prisoners of war to Amun. Winged cobras and sun discs are heavily incorporated into the decoration.

Past this Pylon was the Hypostyle Hall which had 10 chambers on the right side. Five chambers were used to hold treasure and the other five were each dedicated to the following: Ptah (another name of Amun), Sokar (a form of Osiris), Osiris, Ramesses II, and Ramesses III. On the left side was the funeral chamber of Ramesses III, which features the artwork of Thoth inscribing the soul of Ramesses III.

Karnak Temple

Built around 2055 BC, Karnak Temple was dedicated to Atum, Mut, and Khonsu. Together, they were known as the Triad of Thebes. The temple was known as "Ipet-Isu," translated as "the most sacred of places." It is the largest religious building ever constructed and was around 200 acres in size. It can almost be considered a small city built in dedication to the Gods. This was unlike the temples of the Pharaohs and clearly showed that even the mightiest of Pharaohs were still well below the level of power of the Gods. Karnak Temple is large enough to hold St Peter's, Milan, and Nostradamus within itself with room to spare. The Hypostyle hall was 57,000 square feet and boasted 134 columns; it is the largest room ever constructed for religious purposes. The sacred lake was 423 feet by 252 feet. Sacred boats would use the lake during the Festival of Opet.

Luxor Temple

Luxor Temple was built by Amenhotep III around 1390 BC but only finished construction under the reign of King Tutankhamun. Ramesses II added additional structures after its completion. It even had a shrine dedicated to Alexander the Great constructed within it at around 300 BC. The temple has been used as a place of worship from its inception up until the present day. The entrance was a colonnade of seven pairs of columns that stood over 50 feet tall. This led into the Hypostyle Hall, supported by 32 columns, while behind the hall are four smaller chambers and the shrine of Alexander the Great. Luxor Temple was the ending point of the Festival of Opet.

Public Temples

The main purpose of temples in Ancient Egypt was a physical place to house and pray to the Gods. It was widely believed that any fortune or misfortune a person received was directly tied to the whim of the Gods. A city that did not properly tend to the needs of their Gods was thought to be doomed to fall into disarray as the Gods would abandon them to the harshness of the desert that surrounded them. Temples were also used for the ceremony of inaugurating a new Pharaoh and performing the necessary rituals to connect that Pharaoh with the Gods.

Temple Structure

Temples would serve on three levels for Ancient Egyptians. The first service of a temple was to function as a glorious home for a God to dwell in, and as such should be fit for a God to want to live within its walls. Its second service was to serve as a representation of primeval land, an ancient site from which the Gods could have created and shaped the universe. This was the primary reason why there were statues of the Gods within the temples at the inner sanctuaries, raised above the rest of the temple. The third service was to represent the universe and the heavens within a scaled-down, physical form.

Temples were primarily constructed using stone, as it was the most abundant resource available to Ancient Egyptians. Stone was also an ideal choice due to its sturdy nature and overall endurance, as the temples, much like the Gods or the universe, were meant to last until the end of time. Most of the temple's walls were covered with wall reliefs that held scriptures, sculptures, paintings, and other artworks depicting the Gods or the Pharaohs. Many temples had similar features found around or within their design. Obelisks were large monolithic pillars with pointed ends, Pylons served as giant gateways, and inner sanctuaries had altars for offerings to the Gods as well as small statues that could be moved from the altar easily by the priests. Storerooms, courtyards, statues, and hypostyle halls were usually present and very large with many carvings and plants, sacred pools of water for bathing, and fertility prayers were also fairly common. There would be a workshop onsite or nearby for the creation and maintenance of ritual items and temple furniture. Most temples also had an enclosure wall surrounding them to separate them from the rest of the city. It was also common for Egyptians to have small shrines in their households. Common household Gods worshipped included Bes, a guardian of children, and Tauret, a fertility Goddess.

Temple Priests

Ancient Egyptian priests would either serve as full-time or laytime priests. Lay priests would work as a priest for one month every four months and would spend the rest of the year working another profession. Full-time priests would work at the temples year-round. The main priest of each temple was known as the High Priest, and the priest responsible for performing rituals was known as a Waab Priest. Some priests would inherit their jobs through a family lineage of priests, some would be personally appointed by a Pharaoh, and some would buy their way into the priesthood. In any case, being a priest was an honor. High Priests were elected by other priests. Priests were required to be circumcised and to remain celibate while serving as a priest. On duty, priests would live on temple grounds. Priests were not allowed to wear animal products and could only be dressed in linen with plant-based shoes.

Temple Rituals

Ancient Egyptians lived in a polytheistic society where they could worship Gods and Goddesses of their choosing, in most cases, it would be multiple Gods rather than just one. Some Gods were worshipped throughout Egypt, while others were more popular or only popular in a certain city or region. Each town would always have a patron God of the town and a temple dedicated to that God.

Rituals within the temples were done for multiple reasons. One reason was to offer the Gods earthly possessions such as food and clothes to ensure that the Gods had at least basic items available to them. Another reason was to pray for success in a large battle, business venture, crop cycle, or anything else that contained an element of luck. The Gods were thought to provide luck and favor to the followers who worshipped them.

Priests and Pharaohs had daily rituals they had to perform in order to maintain their connection to the Gods. Pharaohs were expected to make daily offerings at the major temples. Priests were expected to use the sacred pools to cleanse themselves multiple times throughout the day. Every morning a priest would need to set the statue of the God in the inner sanctuary on the altar, but first, they would clean it, dress it, and apply makeup to it. The statue would be offered three meals a day. The food would be placed in front of the statue until it was decided that the statue was "fed." The food was then eaten by the priests.

Rituals were also an important aspect of the construction of a temple in order to ensure there was sanctified ground on which to build. Priests would mark off how much space was to be used and would be considered sacred. Priests would also need to be informed of the dimensions of the temple once construction was completed. Priests would place foundation deposits for the temple to be built upon and would also be involved in naming the temple at its consecration.

Festivals

Ancient Egypt would hold many days of celebration throughout the year to give thanks to the Gods; this was known as "Heb."

The Epagomanae

The five extra days at the end of the calendar that Thoth organized for the birth of the five Gods were treated as a celebration of the Gods' birthdays and known as the Epagomanae. Each day was a celebration of Osiris, Horus, Set, Isis, and Nephthys respectively, with offerings made in their name and celebrations held in their honor.

The Festival of Opet

The Festival of Opet took place in the second month of the Ancient Egyptian calendar and could last up to 20 days. The festival was to celebrate the rejuvenation of the Pharaoh by Atum. The festival would begin in the city of Thebes at Karnak Temple, and continue as the Pharaoh traveled to the Luxor Temple in the city of Luxor. This also symbolized the rejuvenation of Atum's power to keep the stability of the universe.

New Year's Day

The new year would begin when the star known as Sothis would disappear from the night sky. This was also a celebration of the death and rebirth of Osiris.

Wadi Festival

Also known as "The Feast of the Valley," a banquet was held to honor the dead. The Wadi Festival took place sometime between Shemu and Akhet and was representative of the strong bond between the living and the dead. Statues of Amun, Mut, and Khonsu would be carried from their temples across the Nile River. Egyptians would also carry images of their deceased loved ones to ensure the safe travels of their souls.

Sed Festival

The Sed Festival was celebrated by a Pharaoh on the 30th anniversary of their reign. This was done to ensure that the Pharaoh was still strongly connected to and in harmony with the Gods. The Pharaoh would run around an enclosed space and then shoot fire arrows in four directions to show that they were the ruler of all sides of the land of Egypt.

These temples and festivals made up a huge part of the daily lives of the average Ancient Egyptian. Whether they were a priest within the temple walls, a craftsman who built for the temples, a farmer who grew food for the temples, a builder who aided in the construction of the temples, a cleaner who maintained the temples, or just as a layperson who worshipped within the temples. These were the places that they could ask for a good harvest, for the blessing of children, for success in a business venture, to find love, to ask forgiveness for a misdeed, or simply to give thanks for all that they had. These were the sacred halls in which Gods and kings resided, and would continue to reside in until the waters of Nun would swallow up the world to begin anew.

Conclusion

From the pages of *Egyptian Mythology*, it can be clearly seen not only how much Ancient Egypt shaped the world of the past, but how much it shaped the world after its glory days and how it continues to shape the world even to this very day. If it didn't then this book would have no reason to exist.

Many of the Ancient Egyptian inventions are still used in our everyday lives. Paper cannot be understated as one of the most important creations in history in terms of recording knowledge. Without sundials and calendars, the very idea of time as we know it would not exist or would at least exist in a completely different fashion from how we currently perceive it. Many of the tales of the Gods and Pharaohs do more than just tell a story of getting from point A to point B. They teach lessons about love, bravery, sacrifice, honor, and duty.

All of this is only a taste of what Ancient Egypt had to offer. All of this is also not giving its sources true justice as Ancient Egypt is not just some story in a book. Almost all of the monuments, artworks, and texts still exist today and are available to the public. Not all of it has remained in Egypt, as many famous pieces of Egyptian Mythology and history now live as exhibits in famous museums around the world. However, many critical pieces of Egyptian Mythology still exist in Egypt, are well preserved and maintained, and serve as a major basis of the Egyptian tourism industry to this day. You don't have to merely read about the Pyramids of Giza or the Ramesseum. You can visit these places in person. You can walk on the same paths that the Ancient Egyptians walked 5000 years ago. You can see what they saw. You can experience their history and their culture firsthand if you are one day privileged enough to visit them yourself.

www.ingramcontent.com/pod-product-compliance
Lightning Source LLC
LaVergne TN
LVHW021735060526
838200LV00052B/3278